TOSEL®

READING SERIES

READING

PRE-STARTER

1

ITC International TOSEL Committee

CONTENTS

About TOSEL®

TOSEL (Test of Skills in the English Language) was developed to meet the demand for a more effective assessment of English as a foreign language for learners from specific cultural settings.

TOSEL evaluates and certifies the proficiency levels of English learners, from the age of 4 through adulthood, along with academic and job performance results.

Background

- Other English tests are ineffective in accurately measuring individual abilities
- Overuse of US-dominated testing systems in diverse cultural and educational contexts in the global English language learning market

Functions & Usage

- Assessment is categorized into 7 levels
- Used as a qualification for academic excellence for school admissions
- Used as a test to assess the English proficiency in the corporate and public sectors

Goals

- Create an effective tool for assessing and evaluating the English skills of English language learners
- Implement efficient and accessible testing systems and methods
- Provide constructive and developmental English education guidance

TOSEL® Strength

LEVELED ASSESSMENTS

An established English test system fit for seven different levels according to learners' cognitive development

ACCURATE DIAGNOSIS

A systematic and scientific diagnosis of learners' English proficiency

EXTENSIVE MATERIALS

Supplementary materials to help learners in an EFL environment to prepare for TOSEL and improve their proficiency

SUFFICIENT DATA

Content for each level developed by using data accumulated from more than 2,000,000 TOSEL test takers delegated at 15,000 schools and academies

CLASSIFIED AREAS OF INTELLIGENCE

Content designed to foster and expand the strengths of each student, categorized by the eight areas of intelligence

CONTINUITY

A complete course of English education ranging from kindergarten, elementary school, middle school, high schoool, and up to adults.

HIGH RELIABILITY

A high reliability level (Cronbach's alpha: .904 for elementary school students / .864 for university students) proven by several studies (Oxford University / Modern Language Journal)

SYSTEMATIC & EFFECTIVE ENGLISH EDUCATION

Accurate diagnosis and extensive materials which provide a step-by-step development in English learning, according to the quality of each learner's ability

TOSEL® Level Chart

Seven Separate Assessments

TOSEL divides the test into seven stages, by considering the test takers' cognitive levels, according to different ages. Unlike other assessments based on only one level, TOSEL includes separate assessments for preschool, elementary school, middle school, high school students, and for adults, which also includes both professionals and college students.

TOSEL's reporting system highlights the strengths and weaknesses of each test taker and suggests areas for further development.

COCOON

Suitable for children aged 4-6 (pre-schoolers)

The first step in the TOSEL system, the test is composed of colorful designs and interesting questions to interest young learners and to put them at ease.

Pre-STARTER

Suitable for children aged 7-8 (1st-2nd grades of elementary school)

Evaluates the ability to comprehend simple vocabulary, conversations, and sentences.

STARTER

Suitable for children aged 9-10 (3rd-4th grades of elementary school)

Evaluates the ability to comprehend short sentences and conversations related to everyday situations or topics.

BASIC

Suitable for children aged 11-12 (5th-6th grades of elementary school)

Evaluates the ability to communicate about personal information, daily activities, future plans, and past experiences in written and spoken language.

JUNIOR

Suitable for middle school students

Evaluates the ability to comprehend short paragraphs, practical texts, and speech covering general topics and to participate in simple daily conversations.

HIGH JUNIOR

Suitable for high school students

Evaluates the ability to use English fluently, accurately, and effectively on a wide range of social and academic subjects, as well as the ability to use sentences with a variety of complex structures.

ADVANCED

Suitable for university students and adults

Evaluates the ability to use practical English required for a job or work environment, as well as the ability to use and understand English at the university level.

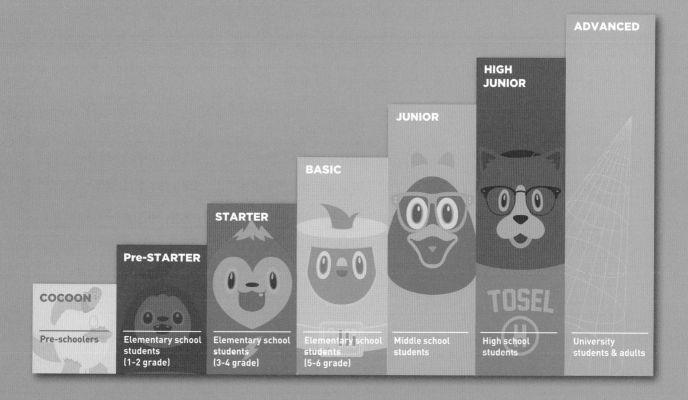

COCOON — Pre-schoolers

Pre-STARTER — Elementary school students (1-2 grade)

STARTER — Elementary school students (3-4 grade)

BASIC — Elementary school students (5-6 grade)

JUNIOR — Middle school students

HIGH JUNIOR — High school students

ADVANCED — University students & adults

Evaluation

Assessing the Four Skills

TOSEL evaluates the four language skills: reading, listening, speaking and writing, through indirect and direct assessment items.

This system of evaluation is part of a concerted effort to break away from materials geared solely toward grammar and reading-oriented education.

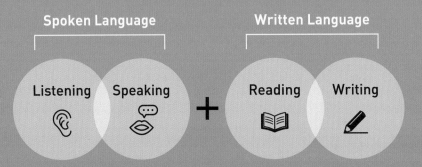

TOSEL Test Information

Level	Score	Grade	Section	
			Section I Listening & Speaking	Section II Reading & Writing
COCOON	100		15 Questions / 15 min	15 Questions / 15 min
Pre-STARTER	100		15 Questions / 15 min	20 Questions / 25 min
STARTER	100		20 Questions / 15 min	20 Questions / 25 min
BASIC	100	1-10	30 Questions / 20 min	30 Questions / 30 min
JUNIOR	100		30 Questions / 20 min	30 Questions / 30 min
HIGH JUNIOR	100		30 Questions / 25 min	35 Questions / 35 min
ADVANCED	990		70 Questions / 45 min	70 Questions / 55 min

Certificates

TOSEL Certificate

The International TOSEL Committee officially evaluates and certifies the level of English proficiency of English learners from the age of 4 to adults.

Certified by

Mar. 2010	Korea University
Dec. 2009	The Korean Society of Speech Science
Dec. 2009	The Korea Association of Foreign Language Education
Nov. 2009	The Applied Linguistics Association of Korea
Oct. 2009	The Pan Korea English Teachers Association

CHAPTER 1

Me & My Family

UNIT 1

I Know My Friends' Names

Teacher's Book
p.44

Who is your best friend?

My name is Tom. Today I start school. I am happy. I see my friends. I know their names. Her name is Sarah. And her name is Emma. He is Liam. She is Sofia. Henry is near Sofia. And I am……? Yes, my name is Tom!

New Words

school

friend

name

happy

Part A. Spell the Words

1.

sc_ool

(A) h

(B) k

(C) p

2.

(A) friends

(B) firedns

(C) fedirns

Part B. Situational Writing

3.

I am _____.

(A) sad

(B) happy

(C) sleepy

4.

Sofia is _____ Henry.

(A) near

(B) behind

(C) far from

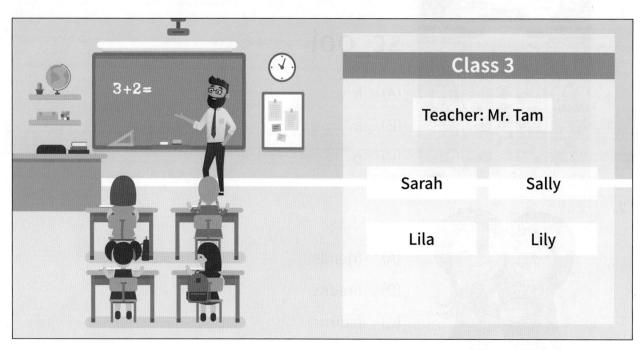

5. Who is the teacher?

(A) Tim

(B) Lila

(C) Mr. Tam

6. Who is NOT in class 3?

(A) Leo

(B) Sally

(C) Sarah

Part D. General Reading and Retelling

My name is Tom. Today I start school. I am happy. I see my friends. I know their names. Her name is Sarah. And her name is Emma. He is Liam. She is Sofia. Henry is near Sofia. And I am······? Yes, my name is _____!

7. What is the best title?

   (A) Tom Has Five Brothers
   (B) Tom Knows Friends' Names
   (C) Tom Does Not Know Names

8. What goes in _____?

   (A) Tom
   (B) Henry
   (C) Emma

9. What day is it?

   (A) Tom's birthday
   (B) Tom's first school day
   (C) Tom's last school day

10. What is NOT true?

   (A) There is no Sarah.
   (B) Henry is near Sofia.
   (C) Tom sees his friends.

Listening Practice

  MP3 PS1-1

 Listen and write.

I Know My Friends' Name

My name is Tom. Today I start ¹_____. I am

²_____. I see my ³_____. I know their names.

Her name is Sarah. And her name is Emma. He is Liam.

She is Sofia. Henry is near Sofia. And I am······? Yes, my

⁴_____ is Tom!

Word Bank

school	hapy
nam	happy
friends	name
skul	flends

 Listen. Pause. Say each sentence.

 MP3 PS1-1G

Writing Practice

 Write the words.

1

s				

2

			n	

Sofia

3

n			

4

h			

 Write the words.

Summary

My name is Tom. Today I start school. I know my new friends'

_____.

Word Puzzle

J	X	G	R	T	I	S	B	Q	S	M	Z	V	A	U
G	Q	A	K	O	L	C	Y	K	W	Z	N	I	F	O
P	W	X	H	Q	L	H	K	D	N	G	A	R	I	M
C	U	B	U	A	D	O	Y	V	W	C	M	V	W	T
F	P	J	U	E	Q	O	S	P	N	Z	E	Q	B	S
R	G	T	Z	H	T	L	F	O	A	V	W	J	M	D
I	L	V	Z	B	G	P	M	Z	D	A	H	U	X	U
E	L	H	C	F	G	G	J	G	T	Z	N	R	Z	W
N	V	T	I	A	C	P	C	R	U	W	E	O	C
D	L	T	K	W	S	A	A	H	I	Z	J	I	V	O
Y	B	H	R	I	N	U	L	A	N	W	O	I	U	B
G	J	R	S	C	G	O	G	P	V	E	P	K	T	B
W	W	Z	C	T	K	B	F	P	E	X	I	K	D	Q
G	N	G	I	K	H	N	H	Y	F	Y	F	X	J	P
I	L	W	I	U	N	A	X	U	X	V	K	J	I	D

🔍 **Write the words. Then find them in the puzzle.**

1 _____   2 _____   3 _____   4 _____

UNIT 2

Maria's Monday

 Teacher's Book p.47

Who is at your school? Draw a picture.

It is Monday. Maria wakes up. She eats breakfast. She says, "Good morning, Mom." She goes to school. It is 9 AM. She sees her English teacher. Her teacher asks, "How are you?" Maria says, "I am fine." Maria eats lunch. She sees her friends. Then she goes home. She talks to her father. She eats dinner. She says, "Good night." Then she goes to sleep.

New Words

7:00 AM
breakfast

noon
lunch

6:00 PM
dinner

wake up

Part A. Spell the Words

1.

_ake up

(A)   h

(B)   s

(C)   w

2.

7:00 AM

(A)   beraksaft

(B)   braketasf

(C)   breakfast

Part B. Situational Writing

3.

Maria sees her _____ teacher.

(A)   art

(B)   math

(C)   English

4.

She goes to _____.

(A)   sleep

(B)   school

(C)   market

5. What day is it today?

    (A) Monday
    (B) Tuesday
    (C) Wednesday

6. Where is Maria at 9 AM?

    (A) home
    (B) school
    (C) cafeteria

Part D. General Reading and Retelling

It is Monday. Maria wakes up. She eats breakfast. She says, "Good morning, Mom." She goes to school. It is 9 AM. She sees her English teacher. Her teacher asks, "How are you?" Maria says, "_____." Maria eats lunch. She sees her friends. Then she goes home. She talks to her father. She eats dinner. She says, "Good night." Then she goes to sleep.

7. What is the best title?

(A) Maria's Family
(B) A Fun Sunday
(C) Maria's Monday

8. What goes in _____?

(A) I have 9.
(B) I am fine.
(C) I like apples.

9. What does Maria do first?

(A) eat breakfast
(B) study English
(C) see her father

10. What does Maria do at home?

(A) eat dinner
(B) cook lunch
(C) study math

Listening Practice

 Listen and write.

  MP3 PS1-2

Maria's Monday

It is Monday. Maria ¹ [_____]. She eats ² [_____].
She says, "Good morning, Mom." She goes to school. It is 9
AM. She sees her English teacher. Her teacher asks, "How
are you?" Maria says, "I am fine." Maria eats ³ [_____].
She sees her friends. Then she goes home. She talks to her
father. She eats ⁴ [_____]. She says, "Good night." Then
she goes to sleep.

Word Bank

breakfast   lunch

wakes up   punch

brakefast   wekes up

diner   dinner

 Listen. Pause. Say each sentence.

  MP3 PS1-2G

✏️ Writing Practice

 Write the words.

7:00 AM

1
| b | | | | | s | |

noon

2
| | | n | | |

6:00 PM

3
| | i | | | |

4
| w | | | | | |

 Write the words.

Summary

Maria goes to _____. She sees her teacher and

her friends. Then she goes home.

N	T	N	C	I	R	D	X	A	X	E	K	B	A	M
U	B	W	I	K	T	S	L	Q	P	W	S	X	F	X
M	E	D	P	Q	D	C	M	H	V	U	R	L	T	E
W	H	B	R	E	A	K	F	A	S	T	S	Q	T	C
E	T	U	J	I	I	B	E	L	M	F	D	L	A	W
X	F	X	R	G	S	S	L	P	J	N	Q	I	U	J
M	P	M	R	T	C	Y	S	L	O	H	D	U	N	V
Y	I	L	D	T	C	S	Z	S	J	D	I	J	E	G
N	Z	P	K	Q	H	C	J	U	B	B	S	V	C	L
P	V	N	J	Y	S	Z	E	K	X	D	G	P	V	U
M	H	V	S	J	A	V	G	I	M	Y	M	W	A	N
G	S	W	A	K	E	U	P	Y	K	Q	R	P	J	C
Z	X	A	Y	W	I	N	F	F	Z	P	J	U	A	H
X	B	M	Z	U	Y	Q	F	D	I	N	N	E	R	O
R	J	Z	N	X	I	P	Z	N	M	Q	O	F	M	P

 Write the words. Then find them in the puzzle.

7:00 AM	noon	6:00 PM	

1 _____   2 _____   3 _____   4 _____

UNIT 3

Family at a Birthday Party

 Teacher's Book p.50

Think! It is your birthday.
What day is it? Who is at your party?

Today is Fadi's birthday. There is a party. Who is there? Fadi's family is there. Fadi's mom and dad are there. Fadi's grandparents are all there. Fadi's uncles are all there. There are three uncles. Fadi's aunts are all there, too. There are two aunts. One cousin is there. But the other cousin is sick. He is not at the party.

New Words

birthday

family

grandparents

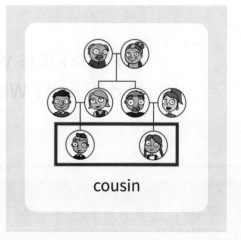

cousin

Part A. Spell the Words

 10 minutes

1.

birt_day

(A) b

(B) d

(C) h

2.

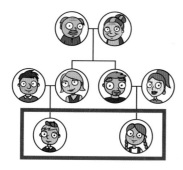

(A) cousin

(B) siocun

(C) niuosc

Part B. Situational Writing

3.

Fadi's _____ come to the party.

(A) friends

(B) teachers

(C) grandparents

4.

One cousin is _____ today.

(A) sick

(B) busy

(C) happy

5. What goes in the blank?

   (A) sister
   (B) cousin
   (C) brother

6. Who is at the top?

   (A) aunt
   (B) uncle
   (C) grandfather

Part D. General Reading and Retelling

Today is Fadi's birthday. There is a party. Who is there? Fadi's family is there. Fadi's mom and dad are there. Fadi's grandparents are all there. Fadi's uncles are all there. There are three uncles. Fadi's aunts are all there, too. There are two aunts. One cousin is there. But the other cousin is sick. He is not at the party.

7. Who is at the party?

(A) Fadi's friends
(B) Fadi's uncles
(C) Fadi's teachers

8. How many aunts are there?

(A) 1
(B) 2
(C) 3

9. Who is sick?

(A) a cousin
(B) an uncle
(C) a brother

10. What is NOT true about the party?

(A) It's Fadi's birthday party.
(B) There are three cousins.
(C) Fadi's parents are there.

Listen and write.

  MP3 PS1-3

Family at a Birthday Party

Today is Fadi's ¹ _____ . There is a party. Who is there? Fadi's ² _____ is there. Fadi's mom and dad are there. Fadi's ³ _____ are all there. Fadi's uncles are all there. There are three uncles. Fadi's aunts are all there, too. There are two aunts. One ⁴ _____ is there. But the other cousin is sick. He is not at the party.

Word Bank

family	cousin
birthday	emily
grandparents	grendparents
cuzin	birsday

 Listen. Pause. Say each sentence.

  MP3 PS1-3G

Writing Practice

 Write the words.

1 | b | | | | d | |

2 | | a | | | |

3 | g | | | d | | a | | | | |

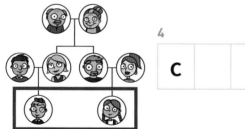

4 | c | | | | |

 Write the words.

Summary

Today is Fadi's birthday party. Fadi's _____ is

at the party. But one cousin is sick.

Word Puzzle

B	K	X	T	Y	H	G	K	Q	D	Z	V	U	H	Q
F	H	V	I	L	I	R	O	E	P	I	L	P	Y	E
B	I	R	T	H	D	A	Y	Z	N	O	H	A	S	P
W	L	R	L	C	J	N	N	R	D	Q	P	J	N	E
R	M	P	L	S	S	D	V	O	L	H	Y	J	Y	Q
W	R	X	O	P	Y	P	F	H	S	A	F	V	A	H
T	H	Q	Q	X	T	A	E	V	C	O	O	Y	H	Q
T	P	A	W	I	O	R	T	B	O	N	X	C	I	B
H	Y	A	F	F	S	E	G	M	U	A	P	G	W	F
K	V	C	A	E	J	N	B	P	S	M	S	G	L	T
G	H	J	M	L	U	T	R	T	I	A	L	E	P	V
D	C	X	I	K	B	S	X	X	N	J	R	F	Z	V
U	O	P	L	D	R	R	A	Q	S	A	K	S	V	W
W	I	R	Y	U	J	I	R	Z	F	E	S	C	S	P
Y	M	B	Z	V	J	J	T	Y	N	L	P	E	J	A

Write the words. Then find them in the puzzle.

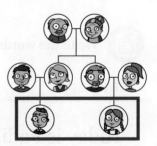

1 _____

2 _____

3 _____

4 _____

UNIT 4

Birthday Gifts

Teacher's Book p.53

Think! What is in the box?
What do you want for your birthday?

It's a birthday! Is it Nina's birthday? No, it's her brother's birthday. Nina's brother is eight years old. He wants soccer shoes. And he wants books. Nina gives him five books. He reads two books today. Next week is Nina's birthday. She does not want books. She wants two robots.

New Words

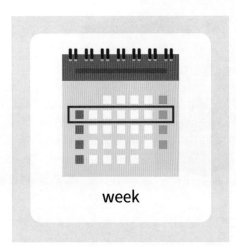

week

soccer

shoes

robot

Part A. Spell the Words

1.
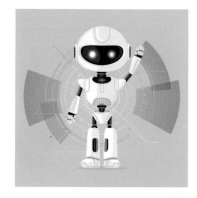

rob_t

(A)   o

(B)   u

(C)   y

2.

(A)   shoes

(B)   sshoe

(C)   sheos

Part B. Situational Writing

3.

Nina's brother gets _____.

(A)   balls

(B)   cake

(C)   books

4.

She likes _____.

(A)   soccer

(B)   baseball

(C)   basketball

5. What day is it?

    (A) his sad day
    (B) his birthday
    (C) his wedding day

6. Count the candles. How old is he?

    (A) seven years old
    (B) eight years old
    (C) nine years old

Part D. General Reading and Retelling

It's a birthday! Is it Nina's birthday? No, it's her brother's birthday. Nina's brother is eight years old. He wants soccer shoes. And he wants books. Nina gives him five books. He reads two books today. Next week is Nina's birthday. She does not want books. She wants two robots.

7. What is the best title?

   (A) Birthday gifts
   (B) Birthday party
   (C) Birthday cakes

8. How old is Nina's brother?

   (A) 8
   (B) 9
   (C) 10

9. What does Nina want?

   (A) a robot
   (B) two books
   (C) two robots

10. How many books does Nina give her brother?

   (A) 2
   (B) 5
   (C) 7

Listen and write.

  MP3 PS1-4

Birthday Gifts

It's a birthday! Is it Nina's birthday? No, it's her brother's

birthday. Nina's brother is eight years old. He wants

[1] _____ [2] _____ . And he wants books. Nina

gives him five books. He reads two books today. Next

[3] _____ is Nina's birthday. She does not want books.

She wants two [4] _____ .

Word Bank

week	woke
soccer	socker
shoes	shuze
robots	lobots

 Listen. Pause. Say each sentence.

  MP3 PS1-4G

✏️ Writing Practice

ABC Write the words.

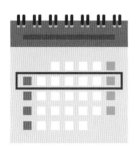

1

w		

2

					r

3

s			

4

	o		

 Write the words.

Summary

It's Nina's brother's birthday. Nina gives him a birthday

_____. Next week is Nina's birthday.

Word Puzzle

S	Q	S	N	I	G	P	D	O	V	U	V	Q	W	W
N	U	D	S	I	U	I	A	J	M	L	U	U	A	S
W	Z	X	U	L	E	L	M	L	S	H	J	J	M	O
J	Q	J	V	W	H	S	G	X	Q	Q	D	L	N	Z
C	N	S	M	E	F	X	L	T	X	F	U	G	A	W
K	M	O	Y	I	E	P	W	G	Y	J	X	G	K	L
R	M	C	S	X	I	Q	T	R	N	Y	R	A	Y	N
A	I	C	M	P	S	V	C	K	O	B	W	E	S	A
A	F	E	J	I	H	G	U	S	T	N	I	B	U	I
Q	M	R	U	J	O	W	G	I	U	M	A	B	C	U
C	D	C	O	Q	E	V	W	M	G	J	C	A	H	B
N	D	R	K	N	S	Y	E	S	A	T	Q	Q	Z	D
N	S	Y	O	Q	V	P	E	Q	N	L	S	L	X	O
F	J	D	Q	W	U	S	K	J	R	O	B	O	T	Z
O	W	Z	V	B	I	W	H	D	A	F	R	J	G	A

 Write the words. Then find them in the puzzle.

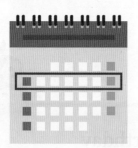

1 _____   2 _____   3 _____   4 _____

CHAPTER REVIEW

 Match the pictures to the correct words.

 birthday

breakfast

cousin

dinner

family

friend

grandparents

happy

lunch

name

robot

school

shoes

soccer

wake up

week

7:00 AM

6:00 PM

CHAPTER 2

A Colorful World

UNIT 5

Color Land

Teacher's Book p.57

Look out the window.
What colors are in the sky?
Name three colors.

We are in Color Land. The sky has many colors. Is it sunny? Then the sky is red. The clouds are yellow. Is it stormy? Then the sky is purple and green. Is it snowy? Then the sky is green! Is it the afternoon? Then the sun sets. The sky is white. Is it night? Then the sky is pink.

New Words

red

yellow

purple

green

Part A. Spell the Words

1.

stor_y

(A) m

(B) n

(C) l

2.

gre_n

(A) a

(B) e

(C) i

Part B. Situational Writing

3.

There are many _____ in the sky.

(A) birds

(B) colors

(C) moons

4.

The clouds are _____.

(A) red

(B) yellow

(C) purple

UNIT 5 Color Land

5. What is this?

    (A) a star
    (B) a cloud
    (C) a rainbow

6. What color is NOT in the picture?

    (A) black
    (B) green
    (C) yellow

Part D. General Reading and Retelling

We are in Color Land. The sky has many colors. Is it sunny? Then the sky is red. The clouds are yellow. Is it stormy? Then the sky is purple and green. Is it snowy? Then the sky is green! Is it the afternoon? Then the sun sets. The sky is white. Is it night? Then the sky is pink.

7. What is the best title?

(A) The Sky of Color Land
(B) The Cars of Color Land
(C) The Animals of Color Land

8. It is a sunny day in Color Land. What color is the sky?

(A) red
(B) blue
(C) yellow

9. It is a stormy day in Color Land. What color is the sky?

(A) gray and red
(B) pink and blue
(C) purple and green

10. When is the sky pink?

(A) morning
(B) afternoon
(C) night

Listen and write.

  MP3 PS1-5

Color Land

We are in Color Land. The sky has many colors. Is it sunny?

Then the sky is ¹_____. The clouds are ²_____.

Is it stormy? Then the sky is ³_____ and green. Is it

snowy? Then the sky is ⁴_____! Is it the afternoon?

Then the sun sets. The sky is white. Is it night? Then the sky

is pink.

Word Bank

yellow	purple
led	porple
yelo	green
red	grin

 Listen. Pause. Say each sentence.

  MP3 PS1-5G

Writing Practice

 Write the words.

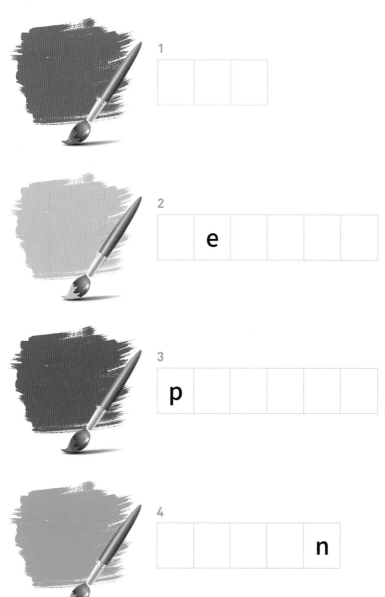

1

2 | | e | | | |

3 | p | | | | |

4 | | | | n | |

 Write the words.

Summary

There are many _____ in Color Land. The sky
and clouds change.

Word Puzzle

B	Y	J	L	M	G	I	A	X	L	G	C	U	H	R
Z	Q	T	A	O	S	D	U	W	E	N	T	Z	Y	T
I	D	K	I	X	Y	T	D	S	R	T	R	U	S	B
L	R	C	G	U	J	S	T	P	V	W	G	P	H	A
V	F	O	Y	C	S	J	R	U	J	N	P	Y	K	W
T	Q	W	V	C	U	U	S	R	T	S	T	D	L	H
K	Q	Q	S	R	H	S	O	P	B	O	T	Q	S	X
J	X	N	Z	T	L	O	Q	L	J	W	U	G	T	F
Y	K	W	U	S	N	G	R	E	E	N	J	Z	Q	D
W	Y	P	N	A	T	A	E	S	V	N	G	Q	O	Y
R	J	K	Y	E	L	L	O	W	U	R	N	M	N	V
E	G	H	L	A	M	F	M	K	W	E	F	N	K	E
D	R	V	X	A	Y	Q	X	I	M	Z	T	A	J	D
G	F	Y	F	H	J	A	T	L	E	I	M	D	P	I
L	W	L	D	Q	R	G	V	Y	A	D	D	N	L	T

 Write the words. Then find them in the puzzle.

1 _____   2 _____   3 _____   4 _____

UNIT 6

 Teacher's Book p.60

So Many Shapes!

Color the circle yellow.
Color the square red.
Color the triangle blue.

There are so many shapes! What is a basketball? What is a baseball? What is a soccer ball? They are circles. What is not a circle? Is a textbook a circle? Is a tall building a circle? No, they are rectangles. What about a triangle? Is there one in our music class? Yes! And a squid is almost a triangle, too!

New Words

circle

rectangle

triangle

squid

Part A. Spell the Words

1.

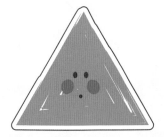

tri_ngle

(A) a

(B) e

(C) w

2.

(A) lid

(B) step

(C) squid

Part B. Situational Writing

3.

A _____ is a circle.

(A) bat

(B) player

(C) baseball

4.

A textbook is a _____.

(A) star

(B) circle

(C) rectangle

5. What shape does the whole pizza look like?

    (A) a circle

    (B) a square

    (C) a triangle

6. What shape does one piece look like?

    (A) a circle

    (B) a square

    (C) a triangle

Part D. General Reading and Retelling

> There are so many shapes! What is a basketball? What is a baseball? What is a soccer ball? They are circles. What is not a circle? Is a textbook a circle? Is a tall building a circle? No, they are rectangles. What about a triangle? Is there one in our music class? Yes! And a squid is almost a triangle, too!

7. What is the best title?

   (A) I Like Circles!
   (B) Give Me Squid!
   (C) So Many Shapes!

8. Which is a circle?

   (A) music
   (B) a baseball
   (C) a textbook

9. Which is a rectangle?

   (A) an egg
   (B) a squid
   (C) a building

10. What is true about a soccer ball?

   (A) It is a circle.
   (B) It has many shapes.
   (C) It is in the music class.

Listening Practice

 Listen and write.

  MP3 PS1-6

So Many Shapes!

There are so many shapes! What is a basketball? What is a baseball? What is a soccer ball? They are 1_____. What is not a circle? Is a textbook a circle? Is a tall building a circle? No, they are 2_____. What about a 3_____? Is there one in our music class? Yes! And a 4_____ is almost a triangle, too!

Word Bank

triangle	circles
trianger	lectangles
rectangles	skwid
squid	serkels

 Listen. Pause. Say each sentence.

 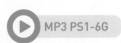 MP3 PS1-6G

Writing Practice

 Write the words.

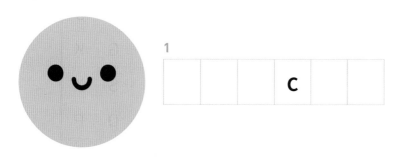

1
| | | | c | | |

2
| r | | | | | g | | |

3
| | | a | | | e |

4
| | | | d | |

 Write the words.

Summary

There are so many _____. Balls are circles.

Books and buildings are rectangles. Squids are almost

triangles.

H	E	T	Z	N	K	M	U	B	A	B	L	J	T	J
K	T	U	G	J	Y	Q	D	M	D	G	G	Z	G	K
R	G	M	S	N	H	F	T	K	T	V	Q	I	S	X
J	Y	E	Z	J	Z	T	R	W	Q	G	D	S	Q	P
C	Y	N	C	T	X	G	E	U	Z	A	Z	G	U	W
F	Z	O	Q	G	I	C	C	R	W	F	L	T	I	Z
C	J	V	X	T	Y	H	T	K	W	X	Z	H	D	D
I	Q	X	B	I	V	M	A	T	V	Y	R	Q	F	M
R	A	E	S	X	B	H	N	T	V	Z	E	D	M	A
C	B	T	K	U	A	G	P	O	F	Q	I	Z	X
L	T	F	K	E	B	I	L	K	S	B	J	J	L	P
E	C	A	G	Y	P	I	E	K	H	Z	V	H	Y	F
K	O	Q	U	S	G	R	H	Z	B	X	O	Q	R	T
O	R	D	O	R	E	K	T	Z	B	I	L	R	X	E
T	R	I	A	N	G	L	E	U	O	M	U	L	O	Y

 Write the words. Then find them in the puzzle.

1 _____   2 _____   3 _____   4 _____

UNIT 7

Teacher's Book
p.63

Animals at the Zoo

What animals are in this picture?
Name three.

Today is Children's Day. Ben and his family go to the zoo. They see many animals. The birds turn their heads. The monkeys wave their arms. The giraffes eat leaves. The elephants play in the water. The seals smile and swim. The donkeys kick with their legs. Ben loves animals. He wants to visit every year.

New Words

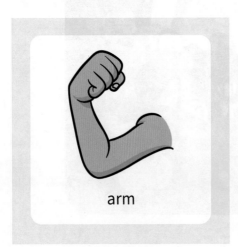

arm

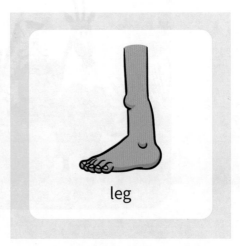

leg

head

zoo

Part A. Spell the Words

1.

lea_

(A)   f

(B)   p

(C)   v

2.

(A)   arm

(B)   ram

(C)   mar

Part B. Situational Writing

3.

The elephants play in _____.

(A)   mud

(B)   sand

(C)   water

4.

Ben is at the _____.

(A)   zoo

(B)   home

(C)   school

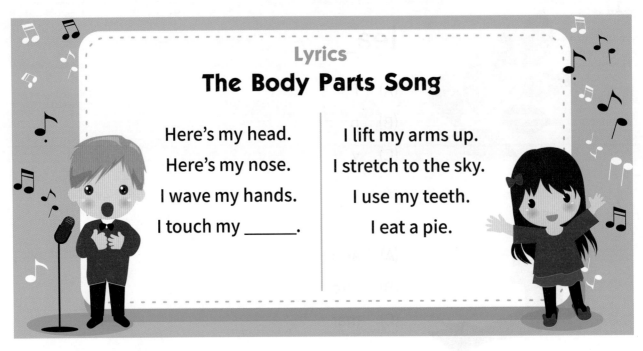

Lyrics

The Body Parts Song

Here's my head.

Here's my nose.

I wave my hands.

I touch my _____.

I lift my arms up.

I stretch to the sky.

I use my teeth.

I eat a pie.

5.

Look at the picture. What word goes in _____?

(A)　toes

(B)　head

(C)　teeth

6.

What does the girl stretch to the sky?

(A)　her feet

(B)　her arms

(C)　her teeth

Part D. General Reading and Retelling

Today is Children's Day. Ben and his family go to the zoo. They see many animals. The birds turn their heads. The monkeys wave their arms. The giraffes eat leaves. The elephants play in the water. The seals smile and swim. The donkeys kick with their legs. Ben loves animals. He wants to visit every year.

7. What is the best title?

   (A) Tired Ben
   (B) Christmas Fun
   (C) Animals in the Zoo

8. What do the giraffes do?

   (A) eat leaves
   (B) play in water
   (C) wave their ears

9. What do the donkeys do?

   (A) run
   (B) kick
   (C) smile

10. Match the animals and their actions.

   birds   •   • kick their legs
   monkeys •   • turn their heads
   seals   •   • swim
   donkeys •   • wave their arms

Listen and write.

 MP3 PS1-7

Animals at the Zoo

Today is Children's Day. Ben and his family go to the

1 _____ . They see many animals. The birds turn their

2 _____ . The monkeys wave their 3 _____ . The

giraffes eat leaves. The elephants play in the water. The seals

smile and swim. The donkeys kick with their 4 _____ .

Ben loves animals. He wants to visit every year.

Word Bank

heads	arms
legs	lags
heds	juice
erms	zoo

 Listen. Pause. Say each sentence.

 MP3 PS1-7G

Writing Practice

 Write the words.

 1

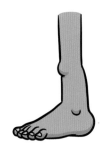 2

 3 | h | | |

 4

 Write the words.

Summary

Ben and his family see many _____ in the zoo.

Ben loves animals.

Z	X	H	E	A	D	I	Z	D	B	E	T	O	H	P
P	B	R	N	R	X	R	O	S	Y	H	T	V	A	T
J	D	M	P	M	C	E	O	T	K	U	K	U	T	Z
A	K	D	K	X	N	U	Z	P	P	D	S	I	Z	R
M	O	V	J	Z	U	G	T	P	J	Y	V	L	C	U
X	K	T	S	E	K	O	Y	F	Y	K	X	K	B	I
X	V	X	I	A	W	B	L	W	R	Z	V	J	K	E
G	P	E	F	Q	N	P	R	C	A	B	T	H	X	B
Q	U	T	V	G	N	V	V	Z	Z	L	V	A	W	Y
V	J	F	Y	E	G	M	J	O	L	E	V	T	G	R
K	U	F	O	P	J	E	G	C	D	G	U	Y	V	C
I	L	V	L	V	Z	T	W	Q	M	E	O	X	K	W
X	Q	V	U	L	I	S	H	B	E	D	F	C	Z	T
G	G	Z	Y	I	V	F	F	B	C	C	C	B	B	Y
P	K	A	B	C	U	X	X	H	U	Q	F	M	W	O

 Write the words. Then find them in the puzzle.

1 _____ 2 _____ 3 _____ 4 _____

UNIT 8

Packing Clothes for Camping

Teacher's Book
p.67

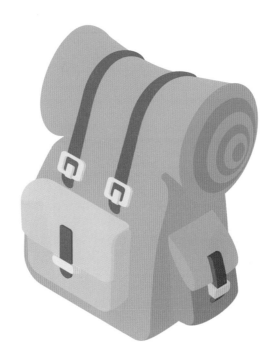

Think! You are going camping.
What clothes do you pack?

Tomorrow I go camping with friends. So now I am packing my clothes. I take a blue bag. I put one brown shirt in the bag. I choose purple pants and a warm green jacket. I pack my yellow socks. I wear a red cap. Now I'm ready for camping!

New Words

shirt

pants

jacket

socks

Part A. Spell the Words

1.

_acket

(A)   j

(B)   z

(C)   s

2.

(A)   locks

(B)   socks

(C)   docks

Part B. Situational Writing

3.

I have a blue _____.

(A)   bag

(B)   bear

(C)   basket

4.

I put on a _____ cap.

(A)   red

(B)   white

(C)   black

5. What is this place?

   (A) a post office
   (B) a fire station
   (C) a clothes shop

6. What can you NOT buy here?

   (A) caps
   (B) shirts
   (C) pants

Part D. General Reading and Retelling

Tomorrow I go camping with friends. So now I am packing my clothes. I take a blue bag. I put one brown shirt in the bag. I choose purple pants and a warm green jacket. I pack my yellow socks. I wear a red cap. Now I'm ready for camping!

7. What is the best title?

   (A) Buying a Bag
   (B) Shopping for Clothes
   (C) Packing for Camping

8. What color are the pants?

   (A) red
   (B) blue
   (C) purple

9. What is green?

   (A) a cap
   (B) a shirt
   (C) a jacket

10. What do I pack?

    (A) pants
    (B) shorts
    (C) shoes

Listening Practice

Packing Clothes for Camping

Tomorrow I go camping with friends. So now I am packing my clothes. I take a blue bag. I put one brown [1]_____ in the bag. I choose purple [2]_____ and a warm green [3]_____. I pack my yellow [4]_____. I wear a red cap. Now I'm ready for camping!

Word Bank

jacket	shert
zecket	pents
pants	shirt
soks	socks

Writing Practice

 Write the words.

1

s			

2

	a		

3

					t

4

s			

 Write the words.

Summary

I am going camping. I pack my _____ in my blue bag.

C	E	Z	C	K	V	X	X	I	P	F	C	L	D	C
Z	W	T	I	G	O	Q	G	S	M	C	Q	N	I	E
U	C	O	Y	J	F	J	B	C	W	H	S	D	I	U
Y	W	F	D	W	U	C	R	J	S	T	P	V	W	O
C	K	K	E	J	R	R	C	B	O	O	B	A	Y	S
Y	D	L	J	T	R	G	K	U	C	D	P	D	T	Q
W	D	N	B	A	K	J	A	C	K	E	T	F	Q	X
A	U	P	V	J	S	U	T	W	S	S	P	K	U	U
C	W	N	R	N	B	O	O	V	E	W	Q	Z	R	O
J	S	O	I	F	R	O	Y	A	Q	P	A	N	T	S
D	N	D	E	K	H	I	M	E	K	W	U	K	Z	V
P	K	Q	C	T	F	D	L	V	R	T	M	P	A	B
X	U	X	F	T	N	E	W	G	O	H	U	P	N	Q
S	R	I	L	X	I	C	I	E	M	E	H	J	X	D
A	C	J	M	U	A	R	S	H	I	R	T	X	T	X

🔍 Write the words. Then find them in the puzzle.

1 _____ 2 _____ 3 _____ 4 _____

CHAPTER REVIEW

 Match the pictures to the correct words.

arm

circle

green

head

jacket

leg

pants

purple

rectangle

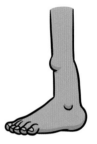

red

shirt

socks

squid

triangle

yellow

zoo

CHAPTER 3

My House

UNIT 9

Linda's New House

Teacher's Book
p.71

Your home has doors.
What color are they?

Linda's family moves to a new house. Linda's mother paints the door. Now it is red. Linda pulls and opens the door. The living room has big windows. Linda's parents are happy. Now they have a large kitchen. There are two bathrooms in the new house. Linda looks at her bedroom. She likes her new room.

New Words

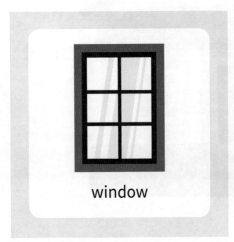

window

kitchen

bathroom

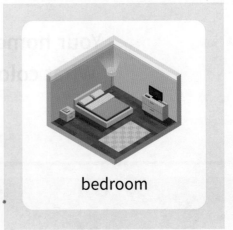

bedroom

Part A. Spell the Words

1.

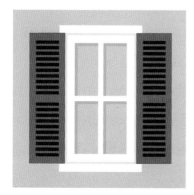

_indow

(A) w

(B) s

(C) h

2.

(A) bathroom

(B) roombath

(C) bothroam

Part B. Situational Writing

3.

The _____ is red.

(A) roof

(B) door

(C) garden

4.

Linda likes her _____.

(A) kitchen

(B) bedroom

(C) living room

UNIT 9 Linda's New House

5. How many bathrooms are in the house?

   (A) 1
   (B) 2
   (C) 3

6. Which of these can you see?

   (A) a door
   (B) a bathtub
   (C) a window

Part D. General Reading and Retelling

Linda's family moves to a new house. Linda's mother paints the door. Now it is red. Linda pulls and opens the door. The living room has big windows. Linda's parents are happy. Now they have a large kitchen. There are two bathrooms in the new house. Linda looks at her bedroom. She likes her new room.

7. What is the best title?

    (A) Linda's Old House
    (B) Linda's New House
    (C) Linda Paints a House

8. Where does the family go?

    (A) to a new town
    (B) to a new house
    (C) to a new library

9. Why are Linda's parents happy?

    (A) The door is blue.
    (B) The kitchen is large.
    (C) There are three bathrooms.

10. What are the windows like?

    (A) big
    (B) dirty
    (C) clean

Listening Practice

Listen and write.

Linda's New House

Linda's family moves to a new house. Linda's mother paints the door. Now it is red. Linda pulls and opens the door.

The living room has big ¹_____. Linda's parents are happy. Now they have a large ²_____. There are two ³_____ in the new house. Linda looks at her ⁴_____. She likes her new room.

Word Bank

windows	windos
kitchen	chicken
bathrooms	bassrooms
bedroom	betroom

Listen. Pause. Say each sentence.

Writing Practice

 Write the words.

1

i

2

n

3

b r

4

b r

 Write the words.

Summary

Linda's family moves to a new _____. Linda's mother paints the door. Linda likes her new room.

Word Puzzle

V	Z	Q	G	Y	J	W	H	Z	V	V	K	D	V	V
R	U	H	I	R	N	C	B	M	H	T	V	V	Y	R
D	M	F	V	E	Y	Q	Y	I	R	D	T	V	V	Z
Y	C	C	D	Q	Q	Y	Z	Q	K	R	D	M	F	P
D	I	L	L	W	U	B	B	A	P	N	O	F	Y	H
W	L	U	C	K	C	C	E	F	C	D	O	T	I	U
J	C	R	M	I	L	M	D	P	X	F	J	G	O	J
G	C	S	U	M	S	M	R	B	N	P	Y	D	R	M
Z	B	A	T	H	R	O	O	M	T	U	K	Z	R	Y
B	V	P	D	J	W	P	O	G	K	I	F	B	K	S
O	J	L	J	N	D	E	M	L	B	C	L	O	J	E
L	V	P	T	F	O	X	G	I	X	J	H	T	Z	S
M	O	K	I	T	C	H	E	N	L	L	P	X	N	S
H	X	T	J	L	E	D	L	I	O	O	V	H	G	R
F	G	H	U	W	I	N	D	O	W	V	D	N	A

 Write the words. Then find them in the puzzle.

   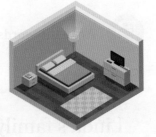

1 _____ 2 _____ 3 _____ 4 _____

UNIT 10

Teacher's Book
p.74

Guess What It Is!

Think of an animal. Is it big or small?
Can it fly? What does it eat? What is it?

It is really long. It has a long, red tongue. It bites, kills, and eats small animals. It does not have arms, legs, or wings. It does not walk, run, or fly. It stays on the ground. Be careful in the forest. Sometimes it hurts people!

New Words

tongue

wing

forest

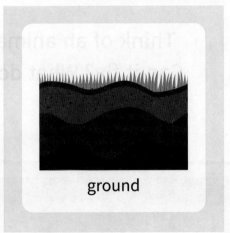

ground

1.

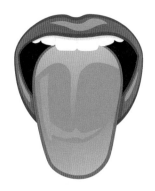

ton_ue

(A)   g

(B)   k

(C)   h

2.

(A)   wings

(B)   ginws

(C)   swing

Part B. Situational Writing

3.

It is in the _____.

(A)   city

(B)   forest

(C)   beach

4.

They cannot _____.

(A)   fly

(B)   run

(C)   stand

5. What animals are in this picture?

(A) lions

(B) tigers

(C) hippos

6. How many crocodiles are there?

(A) 1

(B) 2

(C) 3

Part D. General Reading and Retelling

It is really long. It has a long, red tongue. It bites, kills, and eats small animals. It does not have arms, legs, or wings. It does not walk, run, or fly. It stays on the ground. Be careful in the forest. Sometimes it hurts people!

7. What is it?

(A) a turtle
(B) a snake
(C) a parrot

8. Where does it stay?

(A) in the air
(B) under the sea
(C) on the ground

9. What is true?

(A) It is short.
(B) It has long arms.
(C) It has a red tongue.

10. Where can we read this passage?

(A) in art class
(B) in music class
(C) in science class

Listening Practice

 Listen and write.

  MP3 PS1-10

Guess What It Is!

It is really long. It has a long, red [1]_____ . It bites,
kills, and eats small animals. It does not have arms, legs, or
[2]_____ . It does not walk, run, or fly. It stays on the
[3]_____ . Be careful in the [4]_____ . Sometimes it
hurts people!

Word Bank

wings   forest
ground   winks
forrest   grawnd
tongue   tung

 Listen. Pause. Say each sentence.

 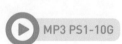 MP3 PS1-10G

Write the words.

1 | t | | | | |

2 | | i | | |

3 | | | | e | | |

4 | g | | | | |

 Write the words.

Summary

A _____ is really long. It has a long, red tongue.

It does not walk, run, or fly.

Word Puzzle

V	M	Q	O	Y	O	S	S	N	G	T	K	I	O	H
O	U	V	F	Y	U	H	W	R	R	Y	F	V	A	D
O	Y	T	O	N	G	U	E	P	O	H	Z	Q	X	G
L	G	Q	R	H	F	G	R	U	U	P	F	M	W	S
M	P	X	E	C	F	L	A	I	N	S	Q	Z	I	L
L	A	K	S	D	N	A	K	E	D	O	Y	O	N	C
O	M	S	T	G	N	Z	J	J	V	R	Y	L	G	W
U	Y	W	Q	D	N	K	Z	D	X	D	G	E	A	Y
H	K	D	Y	G	K	U	N	L	J	F	K	G	V	F
I	D	D	K	U	V	V	H	S	M	D	O	Z	T	O
X	B	P	E	Q	N	Q	N	J	D	K	K	G	M	B
A	L	E	T	A	H	D	R	D	M	W	L	C	H	E
F	T	J	X	W	M	M	R	Y	U	R	D	W	O	W
X	L	P	P	A	J	F	V	W	K	Q	V	N	E	M
O	N	N	E	N	L	I	F	H	N	N	J	U	J	J

 Write the words. Then find them in the puzzle.

1 _____ 2 _____ 3 _____ 4 _____

Teacher's Book p.77

UNIT 11

Sandra's Dad Is a Great Cook!

What is your favorite food?
What do you want for dinner tonight?

Sandra's dad cooks delicious food. This morning, Sandra eats soup and bread. Sandra's sister eats rice and fish. Sandra's dad also makes snacks. Sandra's favorite snack is pizza. Her mother likes hamburgers with cheese the most. Today Sandra's dad tries a new food. It is chicken pasta. Sandra is hungry! She wants chicken pasta right now!

New Words

soup

cheese

pasta

chicken

Part A. Spell the Words

1.

_asta

(A) b

(B) p

(C) f

2.
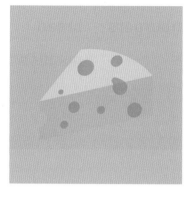

(A) bees

(B) trees

(C) cheese

Part B. Situational Writing

3.

Sandra likes _____.

(A) soup

(B) pizza

(C) bread

4.

Sandra's sister eats _____.

(A) fish

(B) beef

(C) chicken

Meal Plan

	Today	Tomorrow
Breakfast	corn soup	fruit salad
Lunch	hamburgers	bread
Dinner	rice	noodles

5. What does he eat tomorrow?

   (A) rice
   (B) fruit
   (C) soup

6. When are the hamburgers?

   (A) today
   (B) tomorrow
   (C) today and tomorrow

Part D. General Reading and Retelling

> Sandra's dad cooks delicious food. This morning, Sandra eats soup and bread. Sandra's sister eats rice and fish. Sandra's dad also makes snacks. Sandra's favorite snack is pizza. Her mother likes hamburgers with cheese the most. Today Sandra's dad tries a new food. It is chicken pasta. Sandra is hungry! She wants chicken pasta right now!

7. What does Sandra eat for breakfast?

   (A) rice and fish
   (B) rice and pasta
   (C) soup and bread

8. Whose favorite snack is hamburgers?

   (A) Sandra
   (B) Sandra's father
   (C) Sandra's mother

9. How is Sandra right now?

   (A) She is sleepy.
   (B) She is hungry.
   (C) She is very full.

10. What does Sandra want right now?

    (A) fish soup
    (B) chicken pasta
    (C) cheese bread

UNIT 11 Sandra's Dad Is a Great Cook!

Listening Practice

 Listen and write.

Sandra's Dad Is a Great Cook!

Sandra's dad cooks delicious food. This morning, Sandra eats [1]_____ and bread. Sandra's sister eats rice and fish. Sandra's dad also makes snacks. Sandra's favorite snack is pizza. Her mother likes hamburgers with [2]_____ the most. Today Sandra's dad tries a new food. It is chicken [3]_____. Sandra is hungry! She wants [4]_____ pasta right now!

Word Bank

chiken	pasta
sup	chiz
soup	chicken
basta	cheese

 Listen. Pause. Say each sentence.

Writing Practice

 Write the words.

1
| s | | | |

2
| | | e | | |

3
| | | | a |

4
| | i | | | n |

 Write the words.

Summary

Sandra's dad is a great _____. He cooks for

Sandra and her sister. He makes dinner and snacks.

Word Puzzle

U	C	L	R	Q	P	R	R	H	W	M	E	Q	K	K
U	Q	R	B	Y	A	O	Z	A	C	X	A	H	L	G
C	K	J	K	C	S	R	P	X	N	P	Z	S	S	M
Y	H	R	E	Z	T	M	A	B	I	Z	V	O	C	E
Y	C	F	S	W	A	W	R	C	Z	I	P	U	U	Q
U	K	U	J	H	V	F	K	C	K	Z	X	P	W	Y
A	E	E	T	C	I	Y	P	T	L	H	W	J	Q	A
X	U	S	M	I	C	T	O	L	J	P	C	S	Z	P
L	V	L	I	Z	M	R	N	L	J	Y	K	P	C	F
G	D	T	A	C	F	Z	O	V	U	W	O	O	H	A
U	K	Z	J	V	J	A	N	G	E	W	R	S	E	H
W	K	G	R	T	N	A	L	J	N	U	Q	V	E	U
X	Z	L	I	S	F	I	Q	A	L	B	R	V	S	I
G	B	A	Z	Z	W	C	Z	C	H	I	C	K	E	N
C	Z	L	A	N	R	Y	C	C	D	V	F	Z	S	N

 Write the words. Then find them in the puzzle.

1 _____ 2 _____ 3 _____ 4 _____

Teacher's Book p.80

UNIT 12

Lars Loves Music

Can you play a musical instrument?
Which one?

Lars loves music. He likes to listen to the piano. And he likes guitar music. But he can't play the piano or guitar. He can play the violin and cello. He plays them well. His violin is small. His cello is big. Now Lars is learning the drums. He likes the drums. The drums are easy. Lars holds sticks and hits the drums.

New Words

piano

guitar

violin

cello

Part A. Spell the Words

1.

_iolin

(A)   b

(B)   v

(C)   p

2.

g_itar

(A)   i

(B)   u

(C)   e

Part B. Situational Writing

3.

Does Lars play the _____?

(A)   cello

(B)   piano

(C)   drums

4.

Lars plays the drums with _____.

(A)   bats

(B)   sticks

(C)   friends

5. What is NOT in this picture?

    (A) a guitar
    (B) a violin
    (C) a drum

6. What are they doing?

    (A) reading books
    (B) playing baseball
    (C) holding a concert

Part D. General Reading and Retelling

Lars loves music. He likes to listen to the piano. And he likes guitar music. But he can't play the piano or guitar. He can play the violin and cello. He plays them well. His violin is small. His cello is big. Now Lars is learning the drums. He likes the drums. The drums are easy. Lars holds sticks and hits the drums.

7. What is the best title?

   (A) Lars Is a Good Son
   (B) Lars Is a Good Student
   (C) Lars is a Good Musician

8. What can Lars play?

   (A) the violin
   (B) the piano
   (C) the guitar

9. How does Lars play the drums?

   (A) He hits the drums.
   (B) He holds the drums.
   (C) He can't play the drums.

10. What is NOT true?

   (A) Lars has a big cello.
   (B) Lars likes piano music.
   (C) Lars plays the guitar well.

UNIT 12　Lars Loves Music

Listening Practice

 Listen and write.

  MP3 PS1-12

Lars Loves Music

Lars loves music. He likes to listen to the ¹ _____ .
And he likes ² _____ music. But he can't play the
piano or guitar. He can play the ³ _____ and cello. He
plays them well. His violin is small. His ⁴ _____ is big.
Now Lars is learning the drums. He likes the drums. The
drums are easy. Lars holds sticks and hits the drums.

Word Bank

piano	peanow
guitar	gitar
violin	biolin
cello	celo

 Listen. Pause. Say each sentence.

  MP3 PS1-12G

Writing Practice

 Write the words.

1 | | i | | |

2 | g | | | | |

3 | | | o | | |

4 | | | l | |

 Write the words.

Summary

Lars loves _____. He likes to listen to the piano

and guitar. He can play the violin and cello.

Word Puzzle

N	W	P	G	A	M	X	F	A	F	F	K	S	K	W
W	A	I	G	R	J	Y	C	V	T	E	C	F	T	B
G	K	A	W	K	Q	E	Y	E	Y	U	Q	V	O	P
Q	N	N	F	V	V	Q	I	J	G	X	I	K	P	S
G	B	O	F	K	Z	S	T	K	H	D	R	R	Y	N
U	D	U	G	B	D	B	V	M	V	W	N	Y	V	U
I	F	S	B	E	K	L	A	F	U	N	K	F	I	J
T	N	K	T	Q	W	R	X	I	C	E	L	L	O	F
A	Y	X	H	L	T	M	Y	Z	C	O	B	H	L	C
R	D	A	K	J	M	P	Q	Q	F	D	Z	N	I	S
N	M	C	G	H	J	A	B	C	W	V	L	H	N	E
I	F	C	S	U	G	U	F	L	Q	E	C	W	P	V
Q	N	U	O	H	M	U	V	M	L	D	H	V	X	L
G	B	R	S	B	Y	O	Q	W	E	Y	X	V	J	T
M	O	B	E	L	B	K	I	E	F	T	T	B	I	G

 Write the words. Then find them in the puzzle.

1 _____   2 _____   3 _____   4 _____

CHAPTER REVIEW

 Match the pictures to the correct words.

bathroom

bedroom

cello

cheese

chicken

forest

ground

guitar

kitchen

pasta

piano

soup

tongue

violin

window

wing

ANSWERS

CHAPTER 1 | Me & My Family p.10

UNIT 1 — PS1-1 — p.11

	1	2	3	4	5	6	7	8	9	10
⏱	1 (A)	2 (A)	3 (B)	4 (A)	5 (C)	6 (A)	7 (B)	8 (A)	9 (B)	10 (A)
🎧	1 school		2 happy		3 friends		4 name			
✏	1 school		2 friend		3 name		4 happy		📄 names	
✱	1 school		2 friend		3 name		4 happy			

UNIT 2 — PS1-2 — p.19

	1	2	3	4	5	6	7	8	9	10
⏱	1 (C)	2 (C)	3 (C)	4 (A)	5 (A)	6 (B)	7 (C)	8 (B)	9 (A)	10 (A)
🎧	1 wakes up		2 breakfast		3 lunch		4 dinner			
✏	1 breakfast		2 lunch		3 dinner		4 wake up		📄 school	
✱	1 breakfast		2 lunch		3 dinner		4 wake up			

UNIT 3 — PS1-3 — p.27

	1	2	3	4	5	6	7	8	9	10
⏱	1 (C)	2 (A)	3 (C)	4 (A)	5 (C)	6 (C)	7 (B)	8 (B)	9 (A)	10 (B)
🎧	1 birthday		2 family		3 grandparents		4 cousin			
✏	1 birthday		2 family		3 grandparents		4 cousin		📄 family	
✱	1 birthday		2 family		3 grandparents		4 cousin			

UNIT 4 — PS1-4 — p.35

	1	2	3	4	5	6	7	8	9	10
⏱	1 (A)	2 (A)	3 (C)	4 (A)	5 (B)	6 (C)	7 (A)	8 (A)	9 (C)	10 (B)
🎧	1 soccer		2 shoes		3 week		4 robots			
✏	1 week		2 soccer		3 shoes		4 robot		📄 gift	
✱	1 week		2 soccer		3 shoes		4 robot			

CHAPTER 2 | A Colorful World p.44

UNIT 5 — PS1-5 — p.45

	1	2	3	4	5	6	7	8	9	10
⏱	1 (A)	2 (B)	3 (B)	4 (A)	5 (C)	6 (A)	7 (A)	8 (A)	9 (C)	10 (C)
🎧	1 red		2 yellow		3 purple		4 green			
✏	1 red		2 yellow		3 purple		4 green		📄 colors	
✱	1 red		2 yellow		3 purple		4 green			

UNIT 6 — PS1-6 — p.53

	1	2	3	4	5	6	7	8	9	10
⏱	1 (A)	2 (C)	3 (C)	4 (C)	5 (B)	6 (C)	7 (C)	8 (B)	9 (C)	10 (A)
🎧	1 circles		2 rectangles		3 triangle		4 squid			
✏	1 circle		2 rectangle		3 triangle		4 squid		📄 shapes	
✱	1 circle		2 rectangle		3 triangle		4 squid			

UNIT 7 — PS1-7 — p.61

	1	2	3	4	5	6	7	8	9	10
⏱	1 (A)	2 (A)	3 (C)	4 (A)	5 (A)	6 (B)	7 (C)	8 (A)	9 (B)	10 📄
🎧	1 zoo		2 heads		3 arms		4 legs			
✏	1 arm		2 leg		3 head		4 zoo		📄 animals	
✱	1 arm		2 leg		3 head		4 zoo			

UNIT 8 — PS1-8 — p.69

	1	2	3	4	5	6	7	8	9	10
⏱	1 (A)	2 (B)	3 (A)	4 (A)	5 (C)	6 (A)	7 (C)	8 (C)	9 (C)	10 (A)
🎧	1 shirt		2 pants		3 jacket		4 socks			
✏	1 shirt		2 pants		3 jacket		4 socks		📄 clothes	
✱	1 shirt		2 pants		3 jacket		4 socks			

CHAPTER 3 | My House p.78

UNIT 9 — PS1-9 — p.79

	1	2	3	4	5	6	7	8	9	10
⏱	1 (A)	2 (A)	3 (B)	4 (B)	5 (A)	6 (C)	7 (B)	8 (B)	9 (B)	10 (A)
🎧	1 windows		2 kitchen		3 bathrooms		4 bedroom			
✏	1 window		2 kitchen		3 bathroom		4 bedroom		📄 house	
✱	1 window		2 kitchen		3 bathroom		4 bedroom			

UNIT 10 — PS1-10 — p.87

	1	2	3	4	5	6	7	8	9	10
⏱	1 (A)	2 (A)	3 (B)	4 (A)	5 (A)	6 (A)	7 (B)	8 (C)	9 (C)	10 (C)
🎧	1 tongue		2 wings		3 ground		4 forest			
✏	1 tongue		2 wing		3 forest		4 ground		📄 snake	
✱	1 tongue		2 wing		3 forest		4 ground			

UNIT 11 — PS1-11 — p.95

	1	2	3	4	5	6	7	8	9	10
⏱	1 (B)	2 (C)	3 (B)	4 (A)	5 (B)	6 (A)	7 (C)	8 (C)	9 (B)	10 (B)
🎧	1 soup		2 cheese		3 pasta		4 chicken			
✏	1 soup		2 cheese		3 pasta		4 chicken		📄 cook	
✱	1 soup		2 cheese		3 pasta		4 chicken			

UNIT 12 — PS1-12 — p.103

	1	2	3	4	5	6	7	8	9	10
⏱	1 (B)	2 (B)	3 (B)	4 (B)	5 (C)	6 (C)	7 (C)	8 (A)	9 (A)	10 (C)
🎧	1 piano		2 guitar		3 violin		4 cello			
✏	1 piano		2 guitar		3 violin		4 cello		📄 music	
✱	1 piano		2 guitar		3 violin		4 cello			

AI 빅데이터 기반 영어성장 플랫폼
TOSEL® Lab

TOSEL Lab이란?

공동기획
- 고려대학교 문과대학 언어정보연구소
- 고려대학교 공과대학 기계학습 및 빅 데이터연구원
- 국제토셀위원회

**엄선된 100만 명의 응시자 성적 데이터를 활용한
AI기반 데이터 공유 및 가치 고도화 플랫폼**

국내외 15,000여 개 학교·학원 단체응시인원 중 엄선한 100만 명 이상의 실제 TOSEL 성적 데이터와,
정부(과학기술정보통신부)의 연구지원으로 개발된 **맞춤식 AI 빅데이터 기반 영어성장 플랫폼**입니다.

TOSEL Lab Brand Identity

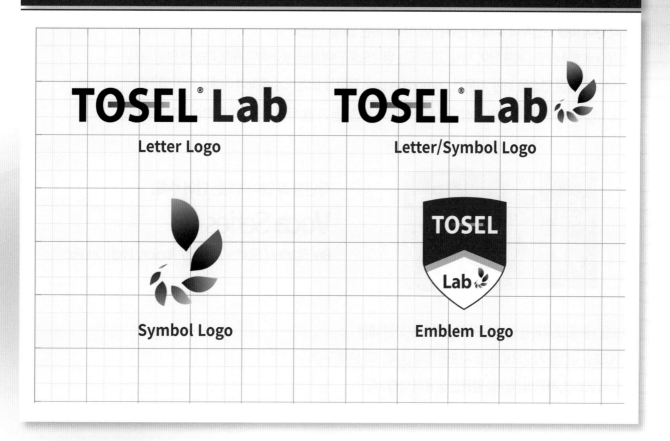

TOSEL Lab에는 어떤 콘텐츠가 있나요?

진단
맞춤형 레벨테스트로
정확한 평가 제공

Placement Test

응시자 빅데이터 분석에
기반한 테스트로 신규 상담
학생의 영어능력을 정확하게
진단하고 효과적인 영어 교육
을 실시하기 위한 객관적인
가이드라인을 제공합니다.

교재
세분화된 레벨로
실력에 맞는 학습 제공

Book Content

TOSEL의 세분화된 교재 레벨
은 각 연령에 맞는 어휘와 읽기
지능 및 교과 과정과의 연계가
가능하도록 설계된 교재들로
효과적인 학습 커리큘럼을
제공합니다.

자기주도학습
교재와 연계한 다양한 콘텐츠로
효과적인 학습 제공

Study Content

Monthly Test를 대비한
다양한 콘텐츠를 제공해 영어
학습에 시너지 효과를 기대할
수 있으며, 학생들의 자기주도
학습 습관을 더 탄탄하게 키울
수 있습니다.

내신과 토셀 고득점을 한꺼번에!

Reading Series

Pre-Starter / Starter / Basic / Junior / High Junior

- 각 단어 학습 도입부에 주제와 관련된 이미지를 통한 말하기 연습
- 각 Unit별 4-6개의 목표 단어 제시, 그림 또는 영문으로 단어 뜻을 제공하여 독해 학습 전 단어 숙지
- 독해&실용문 연습을 위한 지문과 Comprehension 문항을 10개씩 수록하여 이해도 확인 및 진단
- 숙지한 독해 지문을 원어민 음성으로 들으며 듣기 학습, 듣기 전, 듣기 중, 듣기 후 학습 커리큘럼 마련

학년별 꼭 알아야하는 단어 수록!

Voca Series

Pre-Starter / Starter / Basic / Junior / High Junior

- 초등/중등 교과과정 연계 단어 학습과 세분화된 레벨
- TOSEL 시험을 기준으로 빈출 지표를 활용한 예문과 문제 구성
- 실제 TOSEL 지문의 예문을 활용한 실용적 학습 제공
- 실전 감각 향상과 점검을 위한 실전 문제 수록

체계적인 단계별 **문법 지침서**
Grammar Series
Pre-Starter / Starter / Basic / Junior / High Junior

- 초등/중등 교과과정 연계 문법 학습과 세분화된 레벨
- TOSEL 기출 문제 연습과 최신 수능 출제 문법을 포함하여 수능/내신 대비 가능
- 이해하기 쉬운 그림, 깔끔하게 정리된 표와 설명, 다양한 문제를 통해 문법 학습
- 실전 감각 향상과 점검을 위한 기출 문제 수록

한국 학생들에게 최적화된 듣기 실력 완성!
Listening Series
Pre-Starter / Starter / Basic / Junior / High Junior

- 초등/중등 교과과정 연계 말하기&듣기 학습과 세분화된 레벨
- TOSEL 기출 문장과 실생활에 자주 활용되는 문장 패턴을 통해 듣기 및 말하기 학습
- 실제 TOSEL 지문의 예문을 활용한 실용적 학습 제공
- 실전 감각 향상과 점검을 위한 기출 문제 수록

재미와 실력이 **동시에!**
Story Series
Pre-Starter / Starter / Basic / Junior

- 초등/중등 교과과정 연계 영어 학습과 세분화된 레벨
- 이야기 지문과 단어를 함께 연결지어 학생들의 독해 능력을 평가
- 이해하기 쉬운 그림, 깔끔하게 정리된 표와 설명, 다양한 문제, 재미있는 스토리를 통한 독해학습
- 다양한 단계의 문항을 풀어보고 학생들의 읽기, 듣기, 쓰기, 말하기 실력을 집중적으로 향상

교재를 100% 활용하는 TOSEL Lab 지정교육기관의 노하우!

Teaching Materials

TOSEL에서 제공하는 수업 자료로
교재 학습을 더욱 효과적으로 진행!

Study Content

철저한 자기주도학습 콘텐츠로
교재 수업 후 효과적인 복습!

Test Content

교재 학습과 더불어 학생 맞춤형
시험으로 실력 점검 및 향상

Book Content

100만 명으로 엄선된 TOSEL
성적 데이터로 탄생!

국제토셀위원회는 TOSEL Lab 지정교육기관에서 교재로
수업하는 학원을 위해 교재를 잘 활용할 수 있는 다양한
콘텐츠를 제공 및 지원합니다.

**TOSEL Lab 지정교육기관을 위한 콘텐츠로
더욱 효과적인 수업을 경험하세요.**

TOSEL Lab 지정교육기관은

국제토셀위원회 직속 TOSEL연구소에서 20년 동안 보유해온 전국 15,000여 개
교육기관 토셀 응시자들의 영어성적 분석데이터를 공유받아, 통계를 기반으로 한
전문적이고 과학적인 커리큘럼을 설계하고, 영어학습 방향을 제시하여, 경쟁력있는
기관, 잘 가르치는 기관으로 해당 지역에서 입지를 다지게 됩니다.

**TOSEL Lab 지정교육기관으로 선정되기 위해서는
소정의 심사 절차가 수반됩니다.**

TOSEL Lab
더 알아보기

Tel. 02-953-0202
www.lab.tosel.co.kr